THE OFFICIAL
TOTTENHAM HOTSPUR
ANNUAL 2024

Written by Andy Greeves

Designed by Dan Brawn

Contributions by Cathryn Greeves and Justin Cox

A Grange Publication

© 2023. Published by Grange Communications Ltd., Edinburgh, under licence from Tottenham Hotspur Ltd. Printed in the EU.

Photographs © Getty Images & Shutterstock

ISBN 978-1-915879-30-1

CONTENTS

WELCOME TO THE OFFICIAL TOTTENHAM HOTSPUR ANNUAL 2024

Appointed prior to the start of the season, our respective Men's and Women's Head Coaches Ange Postecoglou and Robert Vilahamn were looking to guide their Spurs teams to success during the 2023/24 campaign.

This Annual profiles the star players in both our Men's and Women's squads and introduces summer signings such as Barbora Votíková, Luana Bühler, Guglielmo Vicario, James Maddison and Micky van de Ven.

We take a look at some of the club's top records and honours and there are photographs from our Asia-Pacific Tour during the summer.

Elsewhere, there is a review of eventful seasons for our Men's and Women's teams in 2022/23 and there are also quizzes, games and posters to enjoy - plus plenty more besides.

Enjoy your new Annual and COME ON YOU SPURS!

#COYS

Andy Greeves

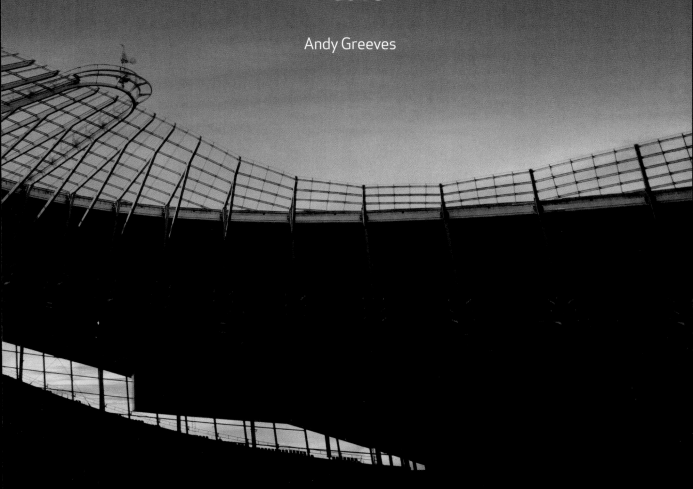

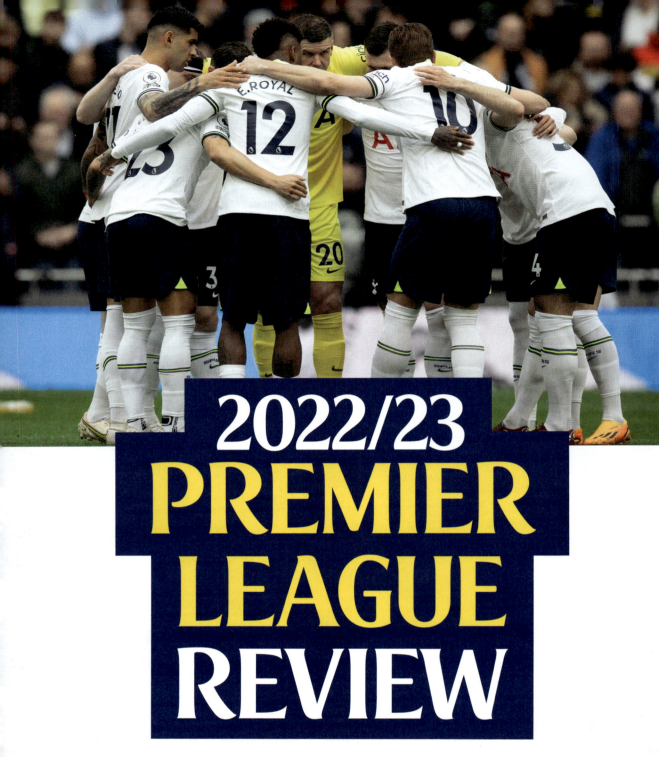

2022/23 PREMIER LEAGUE REVIEW

After another eventful season, Spurs finished in eighth place in the Premier League in 2022/23 with 18 wins, six draws and 14 defeats.

The season started earlier than usual to allow for a planned six-week break for the 2022 FIFA World Cup in November and December. Eleven of our players travelled to Qatar to represent their countries, including Cristian Romero who picked up a winners' medal with Argentina.

Harry Kane became our all-time record goalscorer during the campaign, overtaking the legendary Jimmy Greaves, with his final Spurs tally standing at 280 in all competitions.

AUGUST

Spurs were unbeaten in the Premier League during the month of August, with three wins and two draws giving us a brilliant start to the 2022/23 season. Southampton were defeated 4-1 on the opening day – a game which saw Ryan Sessegnon score the opener and in doing so, bag his first Premier League goal for us. Eric Dier and Dejan Kulusevski also scored and Mohammed Salisu put through his own net.

Kane scored a stoppage time equaliser as we drew 2-2 with Chelsea at Stamford Bridge a week later – a game in which Pierre-Emile Højbjerg opened his account for the season. Our number 10 also netted in a 1-0 win over Wolverhampton Wanderers and bagged a brace in a 2-0 triumph at newly-promoted Nottingham Forest, while a Thilo Kehrer own-goal helped us to a 1-1 draw at West Ham United.

SEPTEMBER

Goals from Højbjerg and Kane gave us a 2-1 win over Fulham at the beginning of September. We were due to travel to Premier League champions Manchester City the following weekend but our match at the Etihad Stadium – along with all other Premier League matches scheduled for that weekend – were postponed due to the death of Queen Elizabeth II.

We returned to Premier League action with an emphatic 6-2 home victory over Leicester City the following weekend. Heung-Min Son got a hat-trick against the Foxes - including an effort which was voted BBC Match of the Day's Goal of the Month - while Kane, Dier and Rodrigo Bentancur were also on target as we extended our unbeaten run in the league to seven games.

OCTOBER

We endured our first Premier League defeat of the season with a 3-1 loss to Arsenal at the Emirates Stadium at the start of October. Kane's converted penalty on 31 minutes drew us level but the Gunners scored twice in the second half to take all three points in a match which saw Emerson Royal sent off.

We then returned to winning ways with a 1-0 triumph over Brighton & Hove Albion as Kane scored his fourth goal in as many Premier League games. The striker was on target from the penalty spot in a 2-0 win against Everton too, while Højbjerg also netted in our home triumph over the Toffees.

We suffered losses at Manchester United (0-2) and Newcastle United (1-2) before coming back from 2-0 down to win at AFC Bournemouth - with substitute Bentancur getting our winner in stoppage time - to end the month on a high.

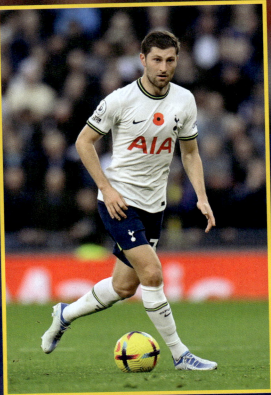

NOVEMBER

We played just two Premier League fixtures in November ahead of the World Cup break. A 2-1 home defeat to Liverpool was followed by a memorable seven-goal thriller against Leeds United which saw us run out 4-3 winners. Goals from Kane, Ben Davies and a brace from Bentancur within two minutes secured our victory.

DECEMBER

Our first Premier League game following the World Cup saw us head to Brentford on Boxing Day where we fought back from 2-0 down to take a point. Kane and Højbjerg scored Spurs' goals in the space of six second-half minutes.

JANUARY

The new year began with defeat against Aston Villa before our supporters who travelled to Crystal Palace three days later were treated to one of our best away performances of the season as we beat the Eagles 4-0. Kane got a brace early in the second half with Matt Doherty and Son also on the scoresheet.

Arsenal claimed the north London bragging rights with a 2-0 victory at Tottenham Hotspur Stadium and we lost 4-2 to Manchester City at the Etihad Stadium four days later. But we won our last league match of January as Kane scored the only goal on the banks of the Thames as we won 1-0 at Fulham.

In the January transfer window, Arnaut Danjuma and Pedro Porro joined the club on loan until the end of the season, from Villarreal and Sporting respectively. Porro's transfer was then made permanent in the summer of 2023.

FEBRUARY

Kane made history on 5 February as he scored the only goal of an entertaining victory against Manchester City at Tottenham Hotspur Stadium to become the club's all-time record goalscorer with 267 strikes. His historic goal came on 15 minutes when Højbjerg found Kane in the box and he drilled a right-footed shot past City 'keeper Ederson. The victory continued our phenomenal run of results against City at Tottenham Hotspur Stadium with five wins out of five in all competitions without conceding a goal!

We were beaten 4-1 at Leicester City the following weekend but goals from Emerson and Son gave us a 2-0 London derby win over West Ham United and we defeated Chelsea by the same scoreline at home a week later. Oliver Skipp scored his first senior goal in our colours to set us on our way before Kane wrapped up all three points against the Blues.

MARCH

We lost 1-0 to Wolverhampton Wanderers early in March before a brace from Kane and a further strike from Son gave us a crucial 3-1 win at home to Nottingham Forest. We followed this victory with a 3-3 draw at Southampton. Pedro Porro scored his first Spurs goal to open the scoring at St Mary's Stadium while Kane and Ivan Perišić were also on target. The game on the south coast proved to be Head Coach Antonio Conte's final game in charge.

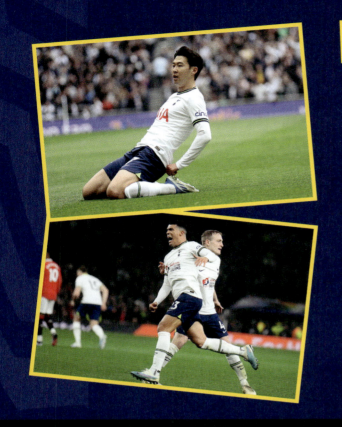

APRIL

April was a busy month with no less than six Premier League matches scheduled. Under caretaker boss, Cristian Stellini, we drew 1-1 with Everton in a game where both sides were reduced to ten men, and beat Brighton 2-1 thanks to strikes from Son and Kane.

We lost to Bournemouth (2-3) and suffered a crushing defeat at Newcastle United (1-6) with Kane's 24th Premier League goal of the campaign at St. James' Park proving to be nothing more than a consolation.

Goals from Son and Porro saw us come from two goals behind to draw 2-2 with Manchester United, with Ryan Mason now in caretaker charge. Three days later, we found ourselves on the wrong end of a seven-goal encounter at Liverpool as Kane, Son and Richarlison scored in our 4-3 defeat.

MAY

A goal from Kane gave us 1-0 victory over Crystal Palace at the start of May. Disappointingly, this was followed by a 2-1 defeat at Aston Villa and 3-1 loss at home to Brentford. But we finished the campaign with a 4-1 win at Leeds United to secure our eighth-place finish. Kane's brace saw him finish second to Erling Haaland in the Premier League goalscoring charts with 30 strikes in 2022/23, while Porro and Lucas Moura were also on target.

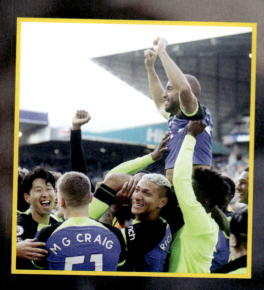

CUP REVIEWS

2022/23 EMIRATES FA CUP & CARABAO CUP

We reached the fifth round of the Emirates FA Cup and the third round of the Carabao Cup in 2022/23.

EMIRATES FA CUP

Third Round Spurs 1-0 Portsmouth

Harry Kane scored the only goal of the game as we saw off League One side Portsmouth in the third round of the FA Cup. It was a quiet first half with few chances for either team, but Kane broke the deadlock five minutes into the second period when he curled the ball into the corner for his 265th Spurs goal.

CARABAO CUP

Third Round Nottingham Forest 2-0 Spurs

Spurs' Carabao Cup campaign in 2022/23 began and ended at the City Ground as Renan Lodi and Jesse Lingard scored for Nottingham Forest within seven second-half minutes to dump us out of the competition. The hosts went down to ten men when Orel Mangala was dismissed with 15 minutes of the match remaining, but despite our best efforts - including Richarlison's late-headed 'goal' which was ruled out for offside - we couldn't find a breakthrough.

EMIRATES FA CUP

Fourth Round Preston North End 0-3 Spurs

A brace from Heung-Min Son helped us to a comfortable win over Preston. He fired home from 30 yards out for our opener on 50 minutes before doubling our advantage from inside the box. Arnaut Danjuma, on loan from Villarreal, came off the bench to score on his Spurs debut for our third of the evening.

Fifth Round Sheffield United 1-0 Spurs

We bowed out of the FA Cup in the fifth round after Sheffield United scored a late winner at Bramall Lane. Richarlison blasted a first-half effort over the bar while Kane, substituted on for the Brazilian on 65 minutes, saw his header go wide. The Championship outfit grew in confidence and, on 78 minutes, Iliman Ndiaye's shot from inside the box found the net to end our cup campaign for another season.

ANOTHER EURO ADVENTURE

CHAMPIONS LEAGUE REVIEW

Our return to the UEFA Champions League in 2022/23 saw us progress to the last 16 of the competition.

GROUP D

Matchday One
Spurs 2 - 0 Marseille

We kicked off our Champions League campaign with a 2-0 victory over Marseille thanks to a brace from 2022 summer signing, Richarlison. The Brazilian headed home with 14 minutes left to play for his first goal in our colours before adding another five minutes later at Tottenham Hotspur Stadium.

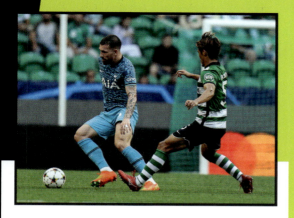

Matchday Two
Sporting CP 2 - 0 Spurs

We were punished by two late goals from Sporting in Lisbon. In a game of few real chances, it looked like we would be taking a point back to north London but a Paulinho header from a corner in the final minute of normal time, followed by a low finish from Arthur Gomes saw the hosts secure victory to remain top of Group D with Spurs in second.

Matchday Three
Eintracht Frankfurt 0 - 0 Spurs

We played out a goalless draw at Eintracht Frankfurt in October 2022, but the scoreline didn't tell the full story. It was an energetic, end-to-end game and Spurs dominated possession for large parts of the match. Harry Kane and Heung-Min Son both saw efforts go wide as Antonio Conte's men missed opportunities to take all three points.

Matchday Four
Spurs 3 - 2 Eintracht Frankfurt

Back in north London, we beat Frankfurt in the reverse match to go top of Group D. The Germans took the lead on the night through Daichi Kamada, but we were soon level through Son. Kane put us in front from the penalty spot on 28 minutes and Son made it 3-1 eight minutes later with a wonderful volley. It was a nervous final few minutes though, as Faride Alidou pulled one back for the visitors with three minutes of the 90 remaining while Kane missed a stoppage-time penalty, but we held on for the win.

Matchday Five
Spurs 1 - 1 Sporting CP

We had to settle for a point against Sporting at home after a last-minute 'goal' from Kane was ruled as offside after a lengthy VAR check. Former Spurs forward Marcus Edwards opened the scoring for the visitors on 20 minutes but we levelled with ten minutes to go when Rodrigo Bentancur headed home from an Ivan Perišić corner.

Marseille 1 - 2 Spurs

A dramatic 2-1 victory at Marseille saw us progress to the last 16 as Group D winners. The hosts struck first through Chancel Mbemba just before the break and at that point we were heading out of the competition. But Clément Lenglet equalised with a header early in the second half and Pierre-Emile Højbjerg hit our winner in the 95th minute to send Spurs through to the knockout phase as group winners.

GROUP D TABLE

		P	W	D	L	GF	GA	GD	PTS
1	Spurs	6	3	2	1	8	6	+2	11
2	E Frankfurt	6	3	1	2	7	8	−1	10
3	Sporting CP	6	2	1	3	8	9	−1	7
4	Marseille	6	2	0	4	8	8	0	6

KNOCKOUT PHASE

Round of 16, first leg
AC Milan 1 - 0 Spurs

Brahim Díaz scored after seven minutes of our round of 16, first leg tie to give Milan a narrow victory at the San Siro. Kane and Eric Dier both had headed chances after Son provided some lovely set-piece deliveries but neither could find the target. Oliver Skipp and Pape Sarr made their first Champions League starts for Spurs with the latter's long-range effort ending up just too close to Milan goalkeeper Ciprian Tătărușanu.

Round of 16, second leg
Spurs 0- 0 AC Milan

A goalless draw with Milan at Tottenham Hotspur Stadium saw us eliminated from the Champions League. We had a couple of chances, but Rossoneri 'keeper Mike Maignan saved Højbjerg's powerful second-half shot and a late headed effort from Kane to send Spurs out of the competition.

TOTTENHAM
HOTSPUR
STADIUM

SAVE 10%
WHEN BOOKING IN ADVANCE

STEP BEHIND
THE SCENES

TOTTENHAM HOTSPUR STADIUM TOURS

BOOK NOW

SPURS
WOMEN'S
SEASON REVIEW 2022/23

The 2022/23 season was Spurs Women's fourth consecutive in the Barclays FA Women's Super League (WSL). We finished ninth in the table following a tough campaign. Highlights included a 1-0 win over Liverpool and a record-breaking 8-0 victory over Brighton & Hove Albion – the team's biggest-ever top-flight win.

The season also saw us reach the quarter-finals of the FA Women's Continental League Cup (Conti Cup) and the fifth round of the Vitality Women's FA Cup. January 2023 signing Bethany England topped our goalscoring charts with 13 strikes in just five months.

SEPTEMBER

Ashleigh Neville's 40-yard strike for our first goal of the season at Leicester City was voted the WSL's Goal of the Month. Her long-range effort was followed by a strike from debutant Drew Spence just before the break to double our advantage. The Foxes halved the deficit courtesy of a Spence own goal but we held on for the win on the opening day of the campaign.

Our other game in September saw Arsenal put four past us with no reply in the north London derby in front of a record WSL crowd of 47,367 at the Emirates Stadium.

OCTOBER

We opened our Conti Cup campaign with a 2-1 victory at Reading. Once again Neville gave us the lead before Nikola Karczewska scored her first goal for the club on the half-hour mark. Our first game at the new home of Spurs Women - Brisbane Road - saw us beat Liverpool 1-0 thanks to an own goal from Niamh Fahey after 11 minutes.

A 3-0 home defeat at the hands of Manchester City was followed with a fantastic display in Brighton where Rehanne Skinner's women won 8-0. Molly Bartrip scored the opener on two minutes before Karczewska doubled our lead. Neville and Spence both scored braces to put us 6-0 up by the hour-mark and substitute Jessica Naz completed our triumph with a double of her own.

NOVEMBER

We bounced back from a 3-0 loss at eventual WSL champions Chelsea with a Conti Cup victory against Coventry United at Brisbane Road. Goals from Eveliina Summanen, Rosella Ayane, Kerys Harrop and Amy Turner saw us take a 4-0 lead before Coventry pulled one back late on. Lenna Gunning-Williams scored on her debut in stoppage time to make it 5-1 to Spurs at the final whistle.

DECEMBER

The only highlight of December proved to be a 1-0 defeat of Southampton in the Conti Cup to make it three wins in three to top our group and progress to the knockout phase. It was Karczewska who scored the only goal of the game.

In the WSL we suffered defeats away at Reading (0-1) and West Ham United (0-2), and at home to Everton (0-3).

JANUARY

January saw the arrival of England international Bethany England from Chelsea. The striker gave Spurs the lead on her debut at Aston Villa but the hosts responded with two quick goals as we went down to a 2-1 defeat.

Chelsea were our opponents in the quarter-finals of the Conti Cup. The Blues' 3-1 victory meant Spence's rocket into the top-right corner in stoppage time at the end of the 90 minutes proved to be just a consolation for us as we were knocked out of the competition.

Four days later we were back to winning ways with a comfortable 5-0 home victory over London City Lionesses in the fourth round of the Women's FA Cup. England and fellow January signing Mana Iwabuchi gave us a 2-0 lead going into the break, before Spence got our third from close range. An own goal from Lionesses captain Harley Bennett made it 4-0 and Summanen rounded off our scoring with ten minutes to go.

FEBRUARY

We went down to a narrow 3-2 defeat against Chelsea at Brisbane Road at the beginning of February. England equalised with a tap-in on 15 minutes after Jess Carter gave the Blues an early lead, but the visitors scored twice more. Karczewska's strike on 88 minutes gave us hope of a late comeback, but it wasn't to be.

An unchanged Spurs Women's side took on Manchester United in front of 21,940 fans at Tottenham Hotspur Stadium the following week – our biggest home crowd of the season. United broke the deadlock through Leah Galton on 67 minutes before a moment of magic from England who cut inside from the left to fire past Mary Earps into the bottom right corner to level the score. An own goal from Bartrip just a minute later gave the visitors all three points.

We bowed out of the FA Cup at the end of the month following a 5-4 penalty defeat to Reading when it finished goalless after extra time in our fifth-round tie.

MARCH

WSL defeats at Manchester City (1-3) which saw Celin Bizet score her first goal for Spurs, and Liverpool, where we went down 2-1 despite going ahead through Ayane, saw Rehanne Skinner depart Brisbane Road and be replaced by her assistant Vicky Jepson as Interim Head Coach.

In Jepson's first game in charge, an outstanding England strike gave Spurs a 1-0 victory over Leicester City and our number 19 was on the scoresheet once more in our 5-1 defeat at home against Arsenal, converting a 38th-minute penalty.

APRIL

Spurs were unlucky not to pick up a point at Everton. Summanen scored our equaliser on 22 minutes after the Toffees went ahead early on. With 90 minutes on the clock, it looked like it would finish with a draw but Aggie Beever-Jones grabbed the winner for Everton in the third minute of stoppage time.

Summanen then bagged a brace in an exciting 3-3 draw against Aston Villa at Brisbane Road, with England getting our third goal of the afternoon. We took a share of the spoils against Brighton at home too as in-form England scored her eighth and ninth goals in 11 games for Spurs to make it 2-2 at Tottenham Hotspur Stadium.

MAY

Defeat at Manchester United (0-3) was followed by a comprehensive 4-1 victory over fellow relegation rivals Reading, to secure Spurs' WSL status. We made a bright start and England opened our account on 29 minutes with a close-range header. Bizet doubled Spurs' lead shortly before half-time and England was on target for her double just after the hour-mark. Kit Graham slid the ball past Grace Moloney in the Reading goal to make it 4-0 before the visitors pulled one back through a Justine Vanhaevermaet header with ten minutes remaining.

We concluded our 2022/23 WSL season with a 2-2 draw at London rivals West Ham. Our top scorer, England, netted twice as we finished the campaign ninth in the table.

ANGE
POSTECOGLOU

Ange Postecoglou became our new First Team Head Coach on 1 July 2023, with the appointment making him the first Australian to manage in the Premier League.

He was born in Athens, Greece on 27 August 1965 but moved to Australia when he was five years old and grew up in Melbourne, Victoria.

He loved football and joined South Melbourne Hellas as a nine-year-old, rising through the youth ranks to play 193 games in defence for their first team between 1984 and 1993. Ange won two championship titles with the club – once in his debut season, then again in 1991.

The left-back also earned four Australia national team caps before a knee injury ended his playing career. He moved into management, taking the top job at South Melbourne in 1996 where he won two league titles.

Ange then led the Australian national Under 17s and Under 20s before moving on to manage in Australia and New Zealand's A-League, winning the Premiership in 2011 and the Championship Grand Finals in 2011

and 2012 with Brisbane Roar ahead of a move to Melbourne Victory.

Renowned for his passion, clarity and personality, Postecoglou became Australian senior national team manager from 2013 to 2017, taking the team to the 2014 FIFA World Cup, winning the AFC Asian Cup in 2015 and securing qualification for the 2018 FIFA World Cup.

He has built teams with an aggressive and assertive style of play who dominate in possession - and that approach has steered his coaching in every task he has taken on.

In 2019, Ange then won Japan's J1 League with Yokohama F. Marinos prior to joining Celtic in 2021. In his debut season, the Australian led the Hoops to the Scottish Premiership and Scottish League Cup and his side went one better in 2022/23 as they retained their league title and won both of Scotland's major domestic cup competitions to claim the treble.

MEN'S FIRST TEAM SQUAD 2023/24

Introducing the stars of our Men's squad.

Details of new signings made during the summer of 2023 can be found on pages 32 and 33 of this Annual.

*Squad correct at time of going to print on 5 September 2023.

Hugo Lloris

Hugo is our record appearance maker of the Premier League era, having represented us 361 times in the division by the end of the 2022/23 season and played in 447 matches for us in all competitions. Signed from Olympique Lyonnais in August 2012, the former France international also has a Club-record number of clean sheets to his name - 127 by the end of the 2022/23 campaign. Born in Nice, Hugo made a record 145 appearances for France between 2008 and 2022 and captained them to their FIFA World Cup triumph in 2018.

GOALKEEPER

Fraser Forster

Fraser joined us from Southampton in June 2022 and made his Spurs debut in our Carabao Cup third round defeat at Nottingham Forest in November that year, while his first Premier League appearance with us came in a 2-2 draw at Brentford the following month. In early 2023, Fraser had a run of nine consecutive matches in our starting line-up after Hugo Lloris suffered a knee injury. He kept a hat-trick of clean sheets during that period against West Ham United and Chelsea in the Premier League and AC Milan in the UEFA Champions League. He made 20 appearances for Spurs in all competitions in 2022/23 and received his first England call up in almost seven years in March 2023.

GOALKEEPER

Ben Davies

A regular for club and country, Ben was just 12 caps short of a century of Wales appearances by the end of 2022/23, while his Spurs record by the end of that season read eight goals in 311 matches. Born in Neath, the defender rose through the ranks at Swansea City to establish himself as a First Team regular. He made 85 senior appearances for the Swans between 2012 and 2014 before his move to us in the summer of 2014. A member of Wales' squads at UEFA Euro 2016 and 2020 as well as the 2022 FIFA World Cup, Ben's 300th match in our colours came in our 2-0 win over Chelsea in February 2023.

Destiny Udogie

Destiny joined us from Udinese in August 2022 and was immediately loaned back to the Serie A side for the 2022/23 season. He had a fine campaign back at the Stadio Friuli, as he scored three times in 34 matches. Having progressed through the ranks at Hellas Verona, Destiny made his professional debut in November 2020. The following year, he joined Udinese on loan - a deal which turned permanent in July 2022. The left-back, who is of Nigerian descent, has been capped by Italy at every level between Under-16 and 21.

Sergio Reguilón

Sergio scored two goals in 67 appearances in his first two seasons with us, having signed from Real Madrid in September 2020 – the same month he made his senior debut for Spain against Ukraine in the UEFA Nations League. The left-back made his first appearance for us in a Carabao Cup match against Chelsea - also in September 2020 - while his Premier League baptism came in our memorable 6-1 away win over Manchester United the following month. He spent the 2022/23 season on loan with Atlético Madrid, for whom he made 12 appearances.

Pedro Porro

Pedro joined us on loan from Sporting in the second half of the 2022/23 season with an obligation for his move to be made permanent in the summer of 2023. Operating down the right flank, Pedro made 17 appearances for us during the 2022/23 season, netting three times in the Premier League against Southampton, Manchester United and in the final day win at Leeds.

Eric Dier

Scoring twice in 42 matches in 2022/23, Eric brought his overall appearances and goals tally for Spurs to 361 and 13 respectively by the end of that campaign. The versatile player then entered his tenth season in our colours in 2023/24, having signed for us from Sporting Lisbon back in July 2014. A dependable figure in either defence or midfield, Eric was one cap short of his 50th England appearance at the time of writing, with the player having previously been included in the Three Lions' squads for UEFA Euro 2016 and both the 2018 and 2022 FIFA World Cups.

Ryan Sessegnon

Ryan made 23 appearances for us in all competitions in 2022/23, scoring twice, until an injury sustained in February 2023 saw him ruled out for the remainder of the campaign. At that point in his career, the left-sided player had featured in 56 Spurs matches since joining us from Fulham in the summer of 2019. Ryan netted 25 times in 120 appearances for the Craven Cottage side between 2016 and 2019 before making his debut for us in a 1-1 draw with Everton in November 2019. He spent the 2020/21 season on loan with Bundesliga side TSG 1899 Hoffenheim.

Japhet Tanganga

DEFENDER

Born in Hackney Japhet started training with us from the age of ten. He progressed through our youth ranks to make his First Team debut against Colchester United in the Carabao Cup in September 2019 which was one of 11 senior appearances he made in our colours that campaign. Japhet followed that up with 13 First Team appearances in 2020/21, 19 in 2021/22 and seven in 2022/23.

Emerson Royal

DEFENDER

Emerson enjoyed a great start to the 2023/24 season as he scored a long-range goal in our 2-2 draw at Brentford. The Brazilian international defender, whose full name is Emerson Aparecido Leite de Souza Junior, signed for us from Barcelona on transfer deadline day in August 2021. The former Ponte Preta, Atlético Mineiro and Real Betis player scored once in 41 appearances in his debut season with us and followed that up with two strikes in 36 Spurs matches in 2022/23.

Djed Spence

DEFENDER

Right-back Djed signed for us from Middlesbrough in the summer of 2022 having spent a successful season-long loan spell at Nottingham Forest the previous campaign. During his time at the City Ground, the former Fulham trainee featured in 46 matches and scored three goals as Forest were promoted to the Premier League via the Championship play-offs. Following six appearances for us in all competitions during the first half of the 2022/23 season, Djed joined French Ligue 1 side Stade Rennais on loan in January 2023 for the remainder of that campaign.

Yves Bissouma

MIDFIELDER

Mali international Yves developed a reputation as one of the Premier League's brightest midfield talents during his four seasons at Brighton & Hove Albion between 2018 and 2022. He netted six times in 124 matches for the Seagulls having joined them from Lille. After swooping to sign the player on a four-year deal in June 2022, Yves made his debut for us against Southampton on the opening weekend of the 2022/23 season – one of 28 matches in which he featured for us during the campaign. An ankle injury sustained against Manchester City on 5 February 2023 kept him out for three months before he returned for our final three matches of the season.

Cristian Romero

DEFENDER

Cristian starred at the 2022 FIFA World Cup, playing in six out of Argentina's seven matches at the tournament, including the final, as La Albiceleste won the competition for the first time since 1986. This during a season in which the centre-back made 34 appearances for us in all competitions. Cristian scored in our 2-2 draw at Brentford on the opening weekend of the 2023/24 Premier League season. His headed goal was his second in our colours, since joining us from Atalanta (originally on loan) in 2021. The defender, who won the Copa America with Argentina in 2021, netted for us for the first time in our 2-0 victory at Brighton & Hove Albion in March 2022.

Pape Matar Sarr

MIDFIELDER

Pape signed for us in August 2021 from Metz and was loaned back to the French club for the 2021/22 season. He made his debut for us off the bench against Aston Villa in a Premier League match on New Year's Day 2023 and made his full debut a week later in our FA Cup win against Portsmouth. He put in a notable appearance alongside Oliver Skipp in a UEFA Champions League round of 16, first leg match against AC Milan in February during a season in which the Senegal international featured in a total of 14 matches in our colours. Pape's first start of the 2023/24 season came in our 2-0 victory over Manchester United in which he scored his first goal for the club.

Tanguy Ndombele

Tanguy joined us from Olympique Lyonnais in July 2019 and scored on his competitive debut in a 3-1 Premier League victory over Aston Villa a month later. The midfielder netted twice in 29 matches in his inaugural season with us and followed that up with six goals in 46 appearances in 2020/21 and two goals in 16 matches in 2021/22. He was loaned back to Lyon in January 2022, where he remained until the end of the season. He then spent the 2022/23 campaign with Napoli, where he scored twice in 40 appearances in all competitions as Gli Azzurri won their first Serie A title since 1990.

Pierre-Emile Højbjerg

A model of consistency since joining us from Southampton in the summer of 2020, Pierre-Emile missed just five of our Premier League matches in his first three seasons as a Spurs player. During that time, he scored ten goals in 145 appearances for us in all competitions. A key player for his country too, the former Bayern Munich, FC Augsburg (loan) and Schalke 04 (loan) man was named in the 'Team of the Tournament' at the delayed UEFA Euro 2020 as he featured in all six of Denmark's matches en route to the semi-finals of the competition.

Oliver Skipp

Truly 'one of our own', Oliver started training with us at the age of five and has progressed through the ranks to become an important member of our First Team squad. Injuries hampered Skippy's progress in 2022/23 as he was ruled out until early October 2022 with a foot problem picked up on our pre-season tour of Korea that summer. But he still managed to feature in 31 matches by the end of the campaign, which brought his overall tally in our colours to 82. A highlight of the season came in February 2023 when he scored a rocket in our 2-0 win over Chelsea!

Rodrigo Bentancur

Rodrigo sustained a serious knee injury in February 2023 that saw him ruled out for the rest of the campaign. Given his influence since joining us from Juventus in January 2022, the Uruguayan was missed in the heart of our midfield. Rodrigo signed for us at the same time as Juve teammate Dejan Kulusevski and both played a big part in us achieving a top four finish in 2021/22. Prior to his injury in 2022/23 meanwhile, he scored six goals in 26 matches, bringing his overall tally to six goals in 44 appearances for Spurs by the end of that campaign.

Giovani Lo Celso

For the second time during his Spurs career, Giovani was loaned to Villarreal during the 2022/23 season, during which time he scored twice in 29 appearances. He previously netted once in 22 matches whilst on loan at El Madrigal in 2021/22. The Argentina international scored twice in 37 appearances whilst on loan with us from Spanish club Real Betis in 2019/20. He put pen-to-paper on a permanent deal with us in January 2020. By the end of the 2021/22 season, Giovani had scored nine goals in 84 matches in our colours. The former Rosario Central and Paris Saint-Germain player was part of Argentina's victorious squad at the 2021 Copa America but missed out on selection for the 2022 FIFA World Cup.

Ivan Perišić

Ivan joined us on a free transfer following the expiration of his contract at Internazionale in July 2022. The experienced Croatia international made 44 appearances in all competitions during his debut season with us in 2022/23, including 33 starts. He played in 34 Premier League matches in his first campaign in the league, which saw him contribute eight assists while he scored in our 3-3 draw at Southampton in March 2023. Capped over 100 times by Croatia, Ivan appeared in the FIFA World Cup Final in 2018 and has league title-winning medals with Borussia Dortmund, Bayern Munich and Inter to his name.

Bryan Gil

Bryan joined us from Sevilla in the summer of 2021 with his debut coming in our UEFA Europa Conference League first leg tie against Paços de Ferreira in August 2021. The Spanish winger went on to make a further 19 appearances in all competitions for us in the first half of the 2021/22 season before being loaned to Valencia for the remainder of the campaign in January 2022. The 2020 Olympic silver medallist headed back to N17 that summer and after playing a further 11 times for Spurs in 2022/23, joined former club Sevilla on loan in January 2023, where he scored twice in 24 appearances and won a UEFA Europa League winners' medal as he started against Roma in the final.

Dejan Kulusevski

After impressing while on an 18-month loan from Juventus, Dejan signed permanently for Spurs in June 2023. He scored five goals in 18 Premier League matches in the second half of the 2021/22 season - his debut campaign - and started 2022/23 in the same form, with a goal and an assist against Southampton on the opening weekend. Injury sidelined the Sweden international on two occasions during his first full season but he still managed 37 appearances in all competitions and netted twice. In December 2022, the Stockholm-born winger - who started his senior career at Atalanta - was awarded the 2022 Guldbollen, the prize for Sweden's best male player. As of June 2023, Dejan has won 30 senior caps and scored two goals.

Richarlison

Richarlison scored three times in 35 appearances in all competitions in his debut campaign with us in 2022/23 after signing from Everton in July 2022. His most notable performance came against Marseille in a UEFA Champions League group match at Tottenham Hotspur Stadium in September 2022 as he scored both our goals in a 2-0 victory. During the 2022/23 season Richarlison – whose full name is Richarlison de Andrade – travelled with Brazil to the 2022 FIFA World Cup in Qatar. His three goals at the tournament included a memorable scissor kick against Serbia in a 2-0 victory. Prior to the start of the 2023/24 campaign, the former Watford and Everton frontman scored a hat-trick in our 5-1 pre-season victory over Lion City.

Heung-Min Son

In August 2023, Sonny was appointed our new Club Captain following a campaign that saw him net 14 times in 47 appearances in all competitions in 2022/23, with one of his most memorable performances seeing him score a 13-minute hat-trick as we beat Leicester City 6-2 in September 2022. The season also saw our number 7 net his 100th Premier League goal on 8 April 2023 in a 2-1 win over Brighton & Hove Albion - the first Asian player to reach that landmark. The previous season, he picked up the Premier League Golden Boot as the division's joint-top scorer after netting 23 times in 2021/22 – a feat matched by Liverpool's Mo Salah. The former Hamburger SV and Bayer Leverkusen player captained South Korea at the 2022 FIFA World Cup in Qatar, leading them to the round of 16 where they were beaten 4-1 by Brazil. He earnt his 111th cap against El Salvador in June 2023.

NEW ARRIVALS

Spurs were busy in the 2023 summer transfer window as the club strengthened their squad by bringing in a number of new players.

Guglielmo Vicario was the first new arrival of the window, with the Italian international goalkeeper moving to north London from Serie A side, Empoli. Born in Udine, he started his professional career at local side Udinese before joining Fontanafredda on loan for a season in 2014. In August 2015 he moved to Venezia, where he made 89 appearances in four seasons, and then he joined Cagliari, who subsequently loaned him out to Perugia and then Empoli in July 2021- a deal which turned permanent the following year.

England international **James Maddison** arrived in N17 from Leicester City. The creative midfielder spent five seasons with the Foxes after signing for them from Norwich City in July 2018. Young Player of the Season winner in his debut campaign with the Foxes, he went on to experience FA Cup glory with Leicester in May 2021 and helped them beat Manchester City in the Community Shield at the start of 2021/22. That season was his most prolific campaign to date as he netted 18 goals and registered 12 assists and followed that up with a further 19 goal contributions in just 30 outings for the Foxes in 2022/23.

Talented young centre-back **Ashley Phillips** also joined us from Blackburn Rovers in August. He started his youth career at National League North side Curzon Ashton before joining Blackburn as a 12-year-old in 2017. He made his first team debut for Rovers in August 2022 aged 17 years and 45 days and departed Ewood Park on the back of making 14 senior appearances.

Manor Solomon spent his early years at Israel-based club Maccabi Petah Tikva ahead of his move to Ukrainian side Shakhtar Donetsk in January 2019, where he gained experience in the UEFA Champions League and won the domestic league title on two occasions, along with the Ukrainian Cup and Ukrainian Super Cup. Manor got his first taste of the Premier League with Fulham when he joined them on loan from Shakhtar Donetsk ahead of the 2022/23 season.

Following an excellent season with Bundesliga side VfL Wolfsburg, **Micky van de Ven** signed for us on a six-year deal in August 2023. Born in Wormer, Netherlands, Micky progressed through the FC Volendam youth ranks to make a total of 48 senior appearances and scoring twice before making his move to Wolfsburg. He had 11 caps for the Netherlands' Under-21 team when he joined us.

Another August addition was highly-rated forward **Alejo Véliz**, who joined us from Rosario Central. Born in Gödeken, Argentina, Véliz made his senior competitive debut for Rosario in July 2021 and went on to feature in 62 matches for the Primera Division side in all competitions, scoring 19 times. Alejo played for Argentina at the FIFA Under-20 World Cup and Under-20 South American Championship in 2023 prior to making his move to N17.

On transfer deadline day on 1 September 2023, Welsh international **Brennan Johnson** joined us from Nottingham Forest. The forward departed the City Ground having scored 29 goals in 109 appearances for Forest between 2019 and 2023. Johnson was selected in Wales' squad for the 2022 FIFA World Cup and appeared in all three of their matches at the tournament.

SPURS WOMEN 2023/24

Introducing the stars of our Women's squad.

Details of new signings made during the summer of 2023 can be found on pages 38 and 39 of this Annual.

Shelina Zadorsky

Our Club Captain originally joined us on loan from Orlando Pride in August 2020 before making the move permanent in January 2021. By the end of the 2022/23 season, she had made over 60 appearances in our colours and was included in Canada's squad for the 2023 FIFA Women's World Cup. Shelina is a two-time Olympic medallist having won bronze with Canada at the 2016 Games in Rio and gold five years later in Tokyo.

Amy Turner

Sheffield-born defender Amy featured in all 22 of our WSL fixtures in her debut season with us in 2022/23 alongside fellow centre-back Molly Bartrip. She signed for us ahead of the campaign from Orlando Pride for whom she made 19 appearances. Capped four times by England in 2015, Amy's previous clubs also include Doncaster Rovers Belles, Leeds United, Liverpool and Manchester United.

Molly Bartrip

For a second season in a row, Molly topped Spurs Women's appearance charts in 2022/23 with only herself, Amy Turner and Angharad James playing in all of our 28 competitive fixtures during the campaign. The Romford-born defender, who joined us from Reading in July 2021, played 27 times in her debut season with us in 2021/22.

Nikola Karczewska

Polish international forward Nikola joined us from French side FC Fleury 91 in July 2022 and netted four times in 18 appearances in all competitions in her debut season with us. One of the most notable performances of her career so far came in April 2022 as she scored two hat-tricks in one game as Poland ran out 12-0 winners against Armenia in a 2023 FIFA Women's World Cup qualifier.

Ellie Brazil

The Nottinghamshire-born forward joined us at the start of the 2022/23 campaign after four seasons at Brighton & Hove Albion. In her debut season as a Spurs player, Ellie sustained an anterior cruciate ligament injury during our WSL fixture against Manchester City in October 2022 which restricted her to just four appearances during the campaign.

Jessica Naz

Former Arsenal player Jessica is one of our longest-serving players, having made the move across north London in 2018. The forward recovered from the setback of missing the 2019/20 season through injury by later being named Women's Young Player of the Year at the London Football Awards in March 2022 during a 2021/22 season that saw her make 21 appearances in all competitions.

Ria Percival

There was a great moment in April 2023 when Ria returned to action as a substitute in a WSL match against Brighton & Hove Albion at Tottenham Hotspur Stadium. The New Zealander, who replaced Bethany England in that game, was able to play her first minutes of football some 366 days on from surgery on an anterior cruciate ligament injury sustained playing for her country against Australia in April 2022.

Ramona Petzelberger

Like Ellie Brazil, Ramona also suffered the disappointment of a long-term injury during her first season with us in 2022/23 and only featured in two games as a result. The German signed for us from Aston Villa in the summer of 2022 on the back of scoring six goals in 30 WSL appearances during her time at Villa. She was welcomed back to training with Ellie in April 2023 as their teammates formed a guard of honour for them as they stepped out onto the pitch.

Celin Bizet Ildhusøy

Having joined us from Paris Saint-Germain in August 2022, Celin was one of the first names on our teamsheet during her debut season, when she featured in 27 matches in total and scored two goals. Born in Frogner, Sørum on October 24 2001, Celin scored on her senior debut for Norway against Armenia in November 2021.

Asmita Ale

A product of Aston Villa's academy, Asmita was a part of the Villans' side that gained promotion to the Barclays FA Women's Super League in 2019/20. The defender helped keep eight clean sheets in the 20 games she played in all competitions in her debut season with us in 2021/22. She followed that up with a further 17 appearances in all competitions in 2022/23.

Bethany England

A January 2023 signing from Chelsea, Bethany enjoyed a dream start to her Spurs career with 13 goals in 14 appearances in the second half of the 2022/23 season. Born in Barnsley, Bethany was named WSL Player of the Season and PFA Women's Players' Player of the Year in 2020 after helping Chelsea win the WSL and FA Women's League Cup. She represented the Lionesses at the 2023 FIFA Women's World Cup.

Angharad James

Midfielder Angharad was one of our most consistent performers in 2022/23 and played in all 28 matches. During the campaign, she earned her 100th international cap for Wales against Slovenia in September 2022 - a game which saw her side qualify for the FIFA World Cup play-offs for the first time in their history.

Kit Graham

In February 2023, Kit returned from a 15-month-long injury layoff as she came on as a substitute in our Women's FA Cup match against Reading. The forward joined us from Charlton Athletic in the summer of 2018 and scored 16 goals in 19 FA Women's Championship appearances in her debut season with us. She followed that up with four strikes in 19 appearances in all competitions in 2019/20 and two goals in 21 matches in 2020/21.

Rosella Ayane

Rosella scored four goals in 24 matches for us in 2022/23 in what was her fourth season in our colours, having joined us from Bristol City in 2019. As of the end of the campaign, the Reading-born forward had 29 Morocco caps and nine senior international goals to her name, having previously represented England at Under-17 and Under-19 level. She made one start and three substitute appearances for Morocco at the 2023 FIFA Women's World Cup.

Becky Spencer

Goalkeeper Becky has made over 60 appearances for us in all competitions since joining from West Ham United in 2019. The stopper, whose previous clubs include Arsenal, Birmingham City and Chelsea, battled with Tinja-Riikka Korpela for the number 1 shirt during the 2022/23 campaign, as she played 13 matches to Korpela's 16. She helped Jamaica reach the last 16 at the 2023 FIFA Women's World Cup.

Drew Spence

Midfielder Drew signed a two-year contract with us in June 2022, with the option to extend for another year, having moved across London from Chelsea. The Jamaica international settled in quickly, scoring five goals in 27 appearances in her debut campaign with us. Along with Becky Spencer, Drew was called up for Jamaica's 23-player squad for the 2023 FIFA World Cup and started all four of their matches at the tournament as the Reggae Girlz made the round of 16.

Eveliina Summanen

Finland international Eveliina made her WSL debut for us against Brighton & Hove Albion in February 2022 – a month after arriving from Swedish side Kristianstad. After featuring in 12 matches in all competitions in the second half of the 2021/22 season, her first full campaign in our colours in 2022/23 saw her score five goals in 25 appearances.

Gracie Pearse

Defender Gracie arrived at the Club in July 2021 after ten years in the Arsenal academy, where she went on to make two senior appearances for the Gunners. She joined FA Women's Championship side Crystal Palace on loan for the 2021/22 season and then spent a portion of the 2022/23 campaign with Bristol City having made three senior appearances for us at the start of the campaign.

Ashleigh Neville

Ashleigh has played over 100 matches for Spurs since arriving from Coventry United in 2017. The full-back became the Club's first ever recipient of the Barclays FA Women's Super League Player of the Month award in February 2022 during a season in which she scored three times in 25 appearances. She followed that up with four goals in 24 appearances in 2022/23.

Eleanor Heeps

Since joining us in August 2021, former England Under-19 international goalkeeper Eleanor has spent two spells on loan with Blackburn Rovers. She joined Coventry United on loan for the 2022/23 campaign.

SPURS WOMEN
SUMMER 2023 ARRIVALS

Spurs Women appointed **Robert Vilahamn** as their new Head Coach in July 2023 on a two-year contract.

Robert began his coaching career in 2008 at Ytterby IS in his homeland and immediately led the side to back-to-back promotions. After a spell as Head Coach of the Under-19 team at Örgryte IS, his next move was to Qviding FIF, where he won promotion in both his seasons in charge.

In 2020, he was appointed Assistant Coach at BK Häcken, helping the side qualify for the inaugural Europa Conference League. Two years later he was appointed Head Coach of the club's women's team, securing Champions League qualification in his first season and reaching the Swedish Cup final in both 2022 and 2023.

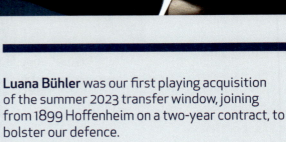

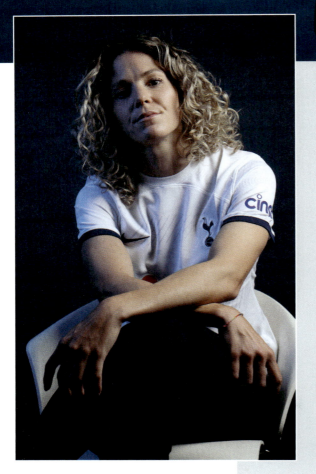

Luana Bühler was our first playing acquisition of the summer 2023 transfer window, joining from 1899 Hoffenheim on a two-year contract, to bolster our defence.

The experienced Swiss international defender began her career with FC Zürich where she played in the UEFA Women's Champions League and was part of the squad that won the Nationalliga A Women as well as the Schweizer Pokal Frauen.

She joined Hoffenheim in 2018 and made 100 appearances in all competitions for the club, scoring six goals. Bühler started for Switzerland in their Group A match against the Philippines at the 2023 FIFA Women's World Cup in Australia and New Zealand, which brought her caps tally to 27 by the end of the tournament.

Our squad was further strengthened with the signing of experienced Finland international **Olga Ahtinen**, who had over 50 senior international caps to her name at the time of her arrival. Born in Kokkola, Ahtinen began her career with her local team, GBK Kokkola, where she made her senior debut in 2013 before spells with Kokkola Futis 10, Pallokissat and PK-35 Vantaa in her homeland. She moved to Danish side Brøndby IF in 2017, with whom she won the Women's Cup in 2018 and the Kvindeliga in 2019. A move to Sweden followed as she signed for IF Limhamn Bunkeflo in 2019 before making the move to Linköpings a year later, where she played 79 games and was named Most Valuable Player in 2022.

Czech international **Barbora Votíková** joined us in August 2023 after a two-year spell at Paris Saint-Germain, where she won the Coupe de France Féminine in 2021/22 and was named Division 1 Féminine Goalkeeper of the Year. Her senior career began at Viktoria Plzeň but it was at Slavia Prague where she really made a name for herself. During her time in the Czech capital, Votíková won four Czech Women's First League titles and the Czech Women's Cup in 2016. She regularly featured in the UEFA Women's Champions League as a Slavia Prague player, reaching the quarter-finals on four occasions while she also reached the competition's last four in her first of two campaigns with Paris Saint-Germain.

Grace Clinton is currently on a season-long loan from Manchester United. The Liverpool-born midfielder, who has been capped by England at Under-17, Under-19 and Under-23 level, joined the Red Devils from Everton in the summer of 2022. She went on to enjoy a successful loan spell with Bristol City during the 2022/23 season, helping the Robins seal promotion back to the WSL as she was named the club's Young Player of the Year in the process.

*New signings correct at time of going to print on 5 September 2023.

THANK YOU!

Whether at home or abroad, Spurs fans are the best in the world and we love having their support!

SPURS ON TOUR

Our Asia-Pacific Tour in the summer of 2023 saw our First Team squad visit Australia, Thailand and Singapore, meeting thousands of adoring fans!

The first stop on the tour was Perth, Australia – a visit which culminated in a friendly match against West Ham United at the Optus Stadium on 18 July 2023 – a fixture watched by 46,266 spectators (match details overleaf). The trip also gave our players the chance to immerse themselves in Australian culture as they checked out the sights in the capital of Western Australia.

Ben Davies, Joe Rodon, Pape Sarr and Davinson Sánchez

visited Kings Park (Kaarta Koomba) - one of the most popular visitor destinations in Western Australia. Offering panoramic views of the Swan River and Darling Range, it is home to over 324 native plant varieties, 215 known indigenous fungi species and 80 bird species. After a tour of the park, the players were treated to a traditional dance and performance, including a local First Nations elder playing a didgeridoo.

Brandon Austin, Pierre-Emile Højbjerg, Tanguy Ndombele, Richarlison and Emerson Royal joined the fun at a coaching clinic for 50 children from three local community clubs at Balcatta FC. Destiny Udogie and Guglielmo Vicario joined our Global Football Development team at Floreat Athena FC to deliver an intimate skills session with children from beneficiaries of Telethon, a charity that supports several initiatives to increase participation in sport for children with disabilities through positive engagement, modified equipment and specialised programme designs.

Our players travelled on from Perth to Bangkok, Thailand, where events in the Thai capital included an Open Training session in front of our fans at the Rajamangala National Stadium. After the session, fans lucky enough to take a place in our 'Golden Circle' were treated to an autograph and selfie session from the whole squad.

Heung-Min Son, Joe Rodon, Pape Sarr and Ivan Perišić met local children from Second Chance Bangkok – an upcycling charity run by residents of Klong Toey – during their time in Thailand. Local children from the charity were invited to the team hotel where our players joined them in an upcycling workshop, turning the previous season's Spurs shirts into new school bags. Meanwhile,

Dejan Kulusevski, Pedro Porro, Emerson Royal and Harvey White joined Thai rock star and long-time Spurs fan, Toon, to taste a number of different Thai food dishes and learn some local language. Toon talked the players through each dish - Pad Thai, Tom Yum, Pad Kra Pao, mango sticky rice, Som Tum and durian.

The final leg of the tour took our players to Kallang, Singapore. There, Destiny Udogie, Guglielmo Vicario, Cristian Romero and Yves Bissouma travelled to Arab Street, where they learned how to make Teh Tarik, a traditional tea consumed in Singapore, Malaysia, Indonesia and India. From there, they took a short trip to the famous Gardens by the Bay, located behind Marina Bay Sands Hotel, to meet with local freestylers Terence Lee and Terry Ong - the 'Urban Street Team' - who showcased

their skills with a Takraw ball and Chapteh shuttlecock before challenging the players to do the same!

While in Singapore, Harry Kane, Eric Dier, Alfie Whiteman, Alfie Devine and Josh Keeley took part in an art session regularly run by the Children's Wishing Well, a charity based in Singapore. They created a Batik piece of art based on our famous cockerel. A long-standing charity partner of AIA, our Global Principal Partner, Children's Wishing Well's aim is to provide opportunities for every child to succeed

in life, regardless of their backgrounds. Elsewhere, Ben Davies and Heung-Min Son attended a charity lunch for our Global Principal Partner AIA's 'Better Lives Fund' at the nearby Conrad Hotel, raising money for charity.

2023/24 PRE-SEASON ROUND-UP

SPURS 2 WEST HAM 3

18 July 2023 | Optus Stadium, Perth

An entertaining back and forth match ended in a narrow defeat to the UEFA Europa Conference League holders in our first pre-season friendly of summer 2023. Ange Postecoglou handed starts to debutants Gugliemo Vicario, James Maddison and Manor Solomon. Despite dominating possession, we were 2-0 down at the break with Danny Ings and Divin Mubama heading home for West Ham within the space of five minutes.

An entirely new XI started the second half which saw a change in tempo as Spurs began to match West Ham's energy. In the 69th minute Giovani Lo Celso pulled one back for us and three minutes later we were level as Destiny Udogie scored his first goal for the club with a header at the far post. But there was disappointment late on as substitute Gianluca Scamacca scored the winner for the Hammers with just over ten minutes remaining.

SPURS 5 LION CITY SAILORS 1

26 July 2023 | Singapore National Stadium, Singapore

Spurs found themselves a goal down after just 15 minutes against Lion City Sailors in the Tiger Cup Final as Shawal Anuar's deft touch was enough to put the ball over Vicario. We thought we had equalised shortly after when Heung-Min Son put the ball in the back of the Sailors' net, but he was caught marginally offside in the build-up. Pape Matar Sarr's thunderbolt of a half volley hit the crossbar and not long after he was brought down in the area, with Harry Kane despatching the resulting penalty to open our account just before half-time.

Postecoglou made a full line-up change at the break once more and three minutes into the second half, the newly-introduced Richarlison volleyed home to give us the lead. The Brazilian

was on target again just four minutes later as a bit of defensive confusion allowed him to head home from inside the six-yard box. Lo Celso finished from close range for our fourth and Richarlison bagged his hat-trick in the dying minutes of the match to complete our rout.

SPURS 5 SHAKHTAR DONETSK 1

6 August 2023 | Tottenham Hotspur Stadium, London

Spurs' first match at home under new boss Postecoglou was a fundraiser for the ongoing humanitarian crisis in Ukraine. In what turned out to be his last game for Spurs, captain for the day Harry Kane scored four times against Shakhtar Donetsk in front of the home fans ahead of his move to Bayern Munich. His opener, on 38 minutes, came from the penalty spot after Maddison was fouled in the area. Shakhtar equalised late on in the first half, with Kevin Kelsy finding a way past Vicario.

Maddison set up Kane for his second of the afternoon on 50 minutes and Kane got his hat-trick five minutes later, put through one-on-one from a Dejan Kulusevski pass. Solomon came on for Son against his former club and created Kane's fourth before Dane Scarlett put the game to bed four minutes into stoppage time.

BARCELONA 4 SPURS 2

8 August 2023 | Estadi Olímpic Lluís Companys, Barcelona

The final match of pre-season ended in defeat against the La Liga champions. Barcelona opened the scoring early on through Robert Lewandowski. We equalised on 24 minutes with an intelligent counter-attacking move. Lo Celso's strike bounced back off the post and Oliver Skipp made no mistake putting the rebound into the back of the net.

Skipp got his second of the afternoon just 12 minutes later to give Spurs the lead and it looked like we might hold on for the victory. But, with ten minutes to go, Barca found an equaliser through Ferran Torres' tidy finish before Marcos Alonso gave the Catalans the lead from a free kick on 90 minutes. Lamine Yamal made sure of Barca's victory with almost the last kick of the game.

WORDSEARCH

Can you find the surnames of EIGHT goalscorers for our men's and women's teams in 2022/23? They can go horizontally, vertically or diagonally, forwards or backwards!

Answers on page 60.

P	K	H	T	D	Y	Q	L	W	M	G	M	Z
O	R	K	U	L	U	S	E	V	S	K	I	C
R	M	X	S	F	Z	Z	T	G	C	D	R	P
R	N	O	V	T	L	X	B	Y	R	N	Y	T
O	N	E	K	N	X	C	K	X	X	A	H	X
K	F	V	N	H	M	L	N	R	C	L	J	N
N	J	F	T	A	N	Q	T	W	L	G	L	F
N	Q	Y	H	Y	M	X	Z	Z	N	N	T	F
C	W	A	D	D	Y	M	J	N	V	E	X	J
N	R	L	N	Y	M	L	U	G	B	G	P	D
G	X	K	N	A	G	G	R	S	D	T	Z	N
X	N	J	R	V	Z	T	R	R	Y	C	T	M
N	O	S	I	L	R	A	H	C	I	R	R	Q

ENGLAND

GRAHAM

KULUSEVSKI

NAZ

PORRO

RICHARLISON

SON

SUMMANEN

CROSSWORD

Can you give the nicknames of some of our fellow Premier League clubs for the 2023/24 season?

Answers on page 60.

ACROSS

2. Newcastle United (7)
5. Luton Town (7)
7. Chelsea (5)
9. Brighton & Hove Albion (8)
10. West Ham United (7)
11. Brentford (4)

DOWN

1. AFC Bournemouth (8)
3. Arsenal (7)
4. Wolverhampton Wanderers (6)
6. Everton (7)
8. Aston Villa (7)

CELEBRATE GOOD TIMES!

SOCK IT TO ME

As Paul Gascoigne ran through to score on his home debut for Spurs against Arsenal in September 1988, his right boot fell off. It mattered not as Gazza slotted home with his stockinged foot before celebrating by kicking an advertising board with his left foot!

DIVE STAR

Jürgen Klinsmann made fun of his 'diver' reputation by celebrating his debut goal for us in a 4-3 win at Sheffield Wednesday by theatrically diving to the floor. His Spurs teammates followed his lead by 'diving' onto the turf in similar fashion!

VEST OF TIMES

David Ginola scored a memorable goal against Barnsley in the FA Cup in 1999 where he slalomed through the Tykes' defence before slotting the ball past goalkeeper Tony Bullock. The Frenchman's celebration saw him remove his match shirt to reveal a plain white vest underneath!

FLIPPING BRILLIANT

During his time at Spurs between 1997 and 2000, José Dominguez would celebrate scoring by performing a series of impressive flips and somersaults. Spurs fans witnessed Dominguez's acrobatics for the first time after he netted against Sheffield Wednesday at White Hart Lane in October 1997.

LET THE GOOD TIMES ROLL

Scoring 122 goals in 306 matches during two spells with Spurs between 2002 and 2011, Robbie Keane had no shortage of opportunities to perform his trademark celebration in front of the Spurs faithful. A cartwheel and forward roll featured in his repertoire, which fans saw time and time again such as when he netted a memorable goal against Blackburn Rovers in March 2006.

FAN-TASTIC

Dele Alli scored two goals in a top of the table clash with Chelsea at White Hart Lane in January 2017. The attacking midfielder celebrated scoring the first of two headers on the night by embracing supporters in the Park Lane end at our former White Hart Lane home.

KING OF HEARTS

For much of his career, including two spells with us from 2007 to 2013 and from 2020 to 2021, Welshman Gareth Bale's signature goal celebration was a heart-shaped symbol he made by putting his hands together after he scored. His celebration and squad number at the time was referenced in an 'eleven of hearts' logo, which Bale trademarked in 2013.

PICTURE THIS

Heung Min-Son also has a famous hand gesture goal celebration, which sees him link his thumbs and index fingers together to make the shape of a camera before putting it to his eye to a 'take a photo'. "The camera celebration is because if I score a goal, it's a good memory," Sonny once explained. "It's like, I take a picture so I have good memories in my mind [of it]."

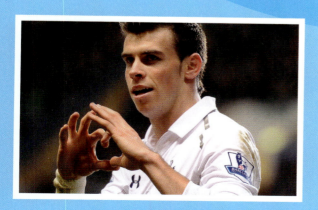

ALSO FEATURING

In addition to being our home ground, Tottenham Hotspur Stadium has also hosted a variety of events besides football matches since opening its doors in 2019…

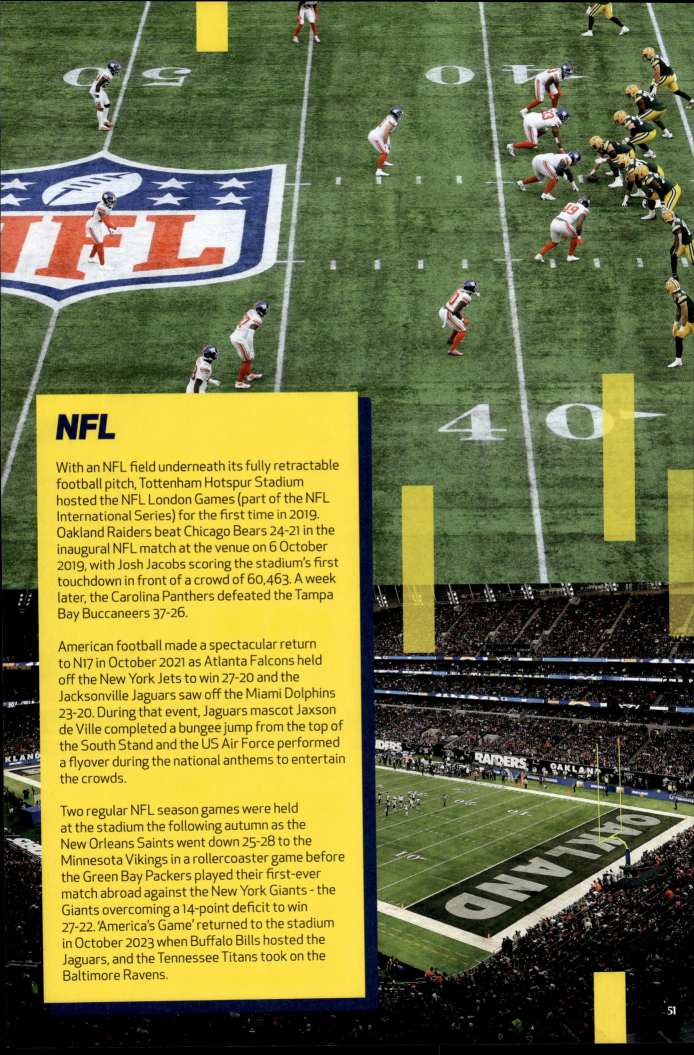

NFL

With an NFL field underneath its fully retractable football pitch, Tottenham Hotspur Stadium hosted the NFL London Games (part of the NFL International Series) for the first time in 2019. Oakland Raiders beat Chicago Bears 24-21 in the inaugural NFL match at the venue on 6 October 2019, with Josh Jacobs scoring the stadium's first touchdown in front of a crowd of 60,463. A week later, the Carolina Panthers defeated the Tampa Bay Buccaneers 37-26.

American football made a spectacular return to N17 in October 2021 as Atlanta Falcons held off the New York Jets to win 27-20 and the Jacksonville Jaguars saw off the Miami Dolphins 23-20. During that event, Jaguars mascot Jaxson de Ville completed a bungee jump from the top of the South Stand and the US Air Force performed a flyover during the national anthems to entertain the crowds.

Two regular NFL season games were held at the stadium the following autumn as the New Orleans Saints went down 25-28 to the Minnesota Vikings in a rollercoaster game before the Green Bay Packers played their first-ever match abroad against the New York Giants - the Giants overcoming a 14-point deficit to win 27-22. 'America's Game' returned to the stadium in October 2023 when Buffalo Bills hosted the Jaguars, and the Tennessee Titans took on the Baltimore Ravens.

CONCERTS

Rock band Guns N' Roses were the first to play a gig at Spurs' new home as they brought their 2020 tour to N17 for two nights in July 2022 – after the original tour dates had been cancelled due to the on-going Covid-19 pandemic. Just under a month later, 86,508 Lady Gaga fans packed out Tottenham Hotspur Stadium over two nights to see the American singer perform on her Chromatica Ball tour. In 2023, Beyoncé put on five amazing shows at the stadium between 29 May and 4 June in front of 238,000 fans as part of her Renaissance World Tour, followed by Red Hot Chili Peppers and Wizkid in July.

BOXING

There have been two huge fights at the stadium as of June 2023. Anthony Joshua, defending his WBA (super), IBF, WBO, and IBO belts, was beaten by the former undisputed cruiserweight champion, Oleksandr Usyk over 12 rounds, in front of a crowd of over 65,000 on 25 September 2021. On 3 December 2022, Tyson Fury defeated Derek Chisora within ten rounds in a one-sided contest in N17. The victory saw him retain his WBC world heavyweight title.

RUGBY UNION

In 2020, Rugby Union side Saracens agreed to play their annual showpiece game at Tottenham Hotspur stadium for the following five years. The first match, scheduled for March 2020, was called off because of Covid-19 so Saracens eventually played their debut fixture at the venue on 26 March 2022 when they beat Bristol Bears 27-23. In 2024, the stadium will host both the European Rugby Champions Cup and European Rugby Challenge Cup Finals.

RUGBY LEAGUE

Rugby League came to Tottenham Hotspur Stadium for the first time on 28 May 2022, as two finals were staged at the venue. Huddersfield Giants took on Wigan Warriors in the 2022 Challenge Cup Final, with Wigan winning 16-14 to lift the cup for the 20th time. The showpiece game had traditionally been played at Wembley Stadium since 1929, but moved to N17 for its 125th anniversary due to Wembley holding the EFL play-offs. The Challenge Cup match was preceded that day by the 2022 RFL 1895 Cup Final, as Leigh Centurions beat Featherstone Rovers 30-16 in the competition for clubs below the Super League.

SIMPLY MAJESTIC!

Spurs-supporting DJ Majestic (Kevin Christie) says he was on "cloud nine" when he had the opportunity to play on the same pitch as some of his all-time heroes in a special charity match in May 2023.

Hi Majestic. Firstly, where does the name 'Majestic' come from?

It's quite a cringe story. My initials are 'K.A.C' (Kevin Adam Christie) and when I first bought my decks when I was 12, my parents let me use the loft as a bit of a space to practise. One day, my dad came upstairs and asked how I was getting on with my new decks and if I had a DJ name sorted. I replied, I'm going to use my initials 'K.A.C', to which my dad replied, 'that's a bad word in another language'. So, I decided 'Majestic' was a much better fit!

How did you become a Spurs fan?

I had no choice in the matter. My Dad was a big Spurs fan, going home and away when he grew up in north London. When I was four or five, to rebel against my dad, I told him I supported Arsenal. He literally packed up a small bag of mine, put it outside the front door of the house and told me to leave! Needless to say, I was 'Tottenham 'Til I Die' from then on!

What are your earliest Spurs memories?

My earliest Spurs memory is the 1991 FA Cup semi-final where Gazza scored that incredible free-kick against Arsenal at Wembley! I recall watching the final at my godfather Nick's house and my dad throwing me in the air when we won! The first game I remember going to was on New Year's Day 1994 against Coventry. We lost 2-1 that day… I remember Darren Caskey scoring our goal!

Are you a Spurs season ticket holder?

I am indeed! I have two tickets in the East Stand and I go as much as I can. If I am in the country and I am not touring I aim to get to every game.

Who are your all-time favourite Spurs players?

There are so many Spurs players I have fallen in love with over the years! From the modern heroes such as Heung-Min Son to the world class

Gareth Bale and my favourite as a kid, Darren Anderton, I could be here all day giving you names… I do have to mention Ledley, who is the King of course!

What have been your best memories supporting Spurs over the years?

Ajax away (UEFA Champions League semi-final, second leg on 8 May 2019) must be up there with the best moment! Getting to the Champions League final that season was incredible and there were some magic moments on the way: Super Jan (Vertonghen) scoring against Dortmund at Wembley and Lucas (Moura) getting the late equaliser at the Camp Nou to see us qualify from the group stages.

What was it like playing for a Celebrity Invitational XI against a Spurs Invitational Charity XI full of club legends in May 2023?

I am still on cloud nine after that day! It was literally a

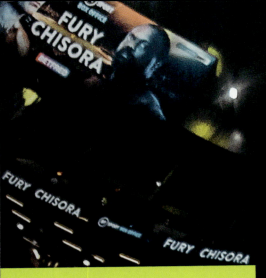

dream come true to share the pitch with some of my all-time favourite players… and they can all still play! When the whistle blew, I ran up to Ledley King, which was a moment I will never forget. I also started singing a famous Dutch song to Edgar Davids in the middle of the pitch, which we both had a chuckle at. Sandro is such a wonderful human being and we had some real fun moments together both on and off the pitch.

You're a DJ of international acclaim and one who reps Spurs through your music we understand?
Yes, I love including Spurs into my music whether it be through lyrical content or whatever. When fellow Spurs fan DJ EZ mixed some Spurs chants into one of our sets together, clips of that went viral online!

Majestic chose his favourite Spurs XI of all-time in a classic 4-4-2 formation >>>

MAJESTIC'S DREAM SPURS XI

H. Lloris

K. Walker   L.King   J.Vertonghen   D. Rose

D. Anderton   L.Modrić   M. Dembélé   G. Bale

H. Kane   D. Berbatov

TOTTENHAM HOTSPUR
RECORDS & HONOURS

CLUB HONOURS

First Division Champions
1950/51, 1960/61
Second Division Champions
1919/20, 1949/50

FA Cup
1901, 1921, 1961, 1962, 1967, 1981, 1982, 1991

UEFA Cup
1971/72, 1983/84

League Cup
1971, 1973, 1999, 2008

EUROPEAN CUP WINNERS' CUP
1962/63

FA Charity/Community Shield
1921, 1951, 1961, 1962, 1967*, 1981*, 1991* (*shared)

CLUB RECORDS

BIGGEST VICTORY

13-2

v Crewe Alexandra (H)
FA Cup Fourth Round
Replay, 3 February 1960

BIGGEST LEAGUE VICTORY

9-0

v Bristol Rovers (H)
Second Division, 22
October 1977

BIGGEST PREMIER LEAGUE VICTORY

9-1

v Wigan Athletic (H)
22 November 2009

MOST GOALS

HARRY KANE

280

goals scored from 2011 through to the end of the 2022/23 season

MOST GOALS IN A SEASON

CLIVE ALLEN

49

goals scored in all competitions during the 1986/87 campaign

MOST APPEARANCES

STEVE PERRYMAN

854

matches played between 1969 and 1986

MOST PREMIER LEAGUE APPEARANCES

HUGO LLORIS

361

from 2012 through to the end of the 2022/23 season

SUPER SPURS QUIZ

Answers on page 61

1. Which suitably-named Spurs forward was named in England's squad for the 2023 FIFA Women's World Cup?

6. At what ground did our Men's team win 4-1 on the final day of the 2022/23 Premier League season?

2. Which national team did Ria Percival play for at the 2023 FIFA Women's World Cup?

7. Which legendary former Spurs player was renowned for his 'dive' goal celebration?

8. Who became the new Head Coach of our Women's team in July 2023?

3. Against which team did Harry Kane score his club record 267th goal in a 1-0 win in February 2023?

9. Which Swiss Women's international defender did we sign from TSG 1899 Hoffenheim Frauen in July 2023?

4. By what score line did our Women's team beat Brighton & Hove Albion in the FA Women's Super League (WSL) in October 2022?

10. From which club did we sign James Maddison in the summer of 2023?

5. What nationality is our Men's team's Head Coach, Ange Postecoglou?

11. In which Australian city did we play a friendly match against West Ham United in July 2023?

12. In what country did we face Lion City Sailors in a friendly match in July 2023?

13. Which position does Guglielmo Vicario play?

14. Who did we face in the first match of the 2023/24 Premier League season?

15. What is the name of the attraction at Tottenham Hotspur Stadium that sees participants ascend 42m to the top of the South Stand roof?

16. Who were the first band to play a gig at Tottenham Hotspur Stadium in July 2022?

17. What nationality is Pedro Porro?

18. Which American singer performed for five nights at Tottenham Hotspur Stadium as part of her Renaissance World Tour in the summer of 2023, attracting over 230,000 fans to N17 in the process?

19. From which Italian club did we complete the permanent signing of Dejan Kulusevski in the summer of 2023?

20. What was the Football League Cup known as when we won it in 2008?

WORDSEARCH

P	K	H	T	D	Y	Q	L	W	M	G	M	Z
O	R	K	U	L	U	S	E	V	S	K	I	C
R	M	X	S	F	Z	Z	T	G	C	D	R	P
R	N	O	V	T	L	X	B	Y	R	N	Y	T
O	N	E	K	N	X	C	K	X	X	A	H	X
K	F	V	N	H	M	L	N	R	C	L	J	N
N	J	F	T	A	N	Q	T	W	L	G	L	F
N	Q	Y	H	Y	M	X	Z	Z	N	N	T	F
C	W	A	D	D	Y	M	J	N	V	E	X	J
N	R	L	N	Y	M	L	U	G	B	G	P	D
G	X	K	N	A	G	G	R	S	D	T	Z	N
X	N	J	R	V	Z	T	R	R	Y	C	T	M
N	O	S	I	L	R	A	H	C	I	R	R	Q

CROSSWORD

Across:
2. MAGPIES
5. HATTERS
7. BLUES
9. SEAGULLS
10. HAMMERS
11. BEES

Down:
1. CHERRIES
3. GUNNERS
4. WOLVES
6. TOFFEES
8. VILLANS

SUPER SPURS QUIZ

1. BETHANY ENGLAND
2. NEW ZEALAND
3. MANCHESTER CITY
4. 8-0
5. AUSTRALIAN
6. ELLAND ROAD
   (HOME OF LEEDS UNITED)
7. JÜRGEN KLINSMANN
8. ROBERT VILAHAMN
9. LUANA BÜHLER
10. LEICESTER CITY
11. PERTH
12. SINGAPORE
13. GOALKEEPER
14. BRENTFORD
15. THE DARE SKYWALK
16. GUNS N' ROSES
17. SPANISH
18. BEYONCÉ
19. JUVENTUS
20. CARLING CUP